French Bistro Cooking

Easy Classic French Cuisine Recipes to Make at Home

Sarah Spencer

Disclaimer and Terms of Use

Effort has been made to ensure that the information in this book is accurate and complete. However, the author and the publisher do not warrant the accuracy of the information, text, and graphics contained within the book due to the rapidly changing nature of science, research, known and unknown facts, and internet. The author and the publisher do not hold any responsibility for errors, omissions, or contrary interpretation of the subject matter herein. This book is presented solely for motivational and informational purposes only.

The recipes provided in this book are for informational purposes only and are not intended to provide dietary advice. A medical practitioner should be consulted before making any changes in diet. Additionally, recipe cooking times may require adjustment depending on age and quality of appliances. Readers are strongly urged to take all precautions to ensure ingredients are fully cooked in order to avoid the dangers of foodborne illnesses. The recipes and suggestions provided in this book are solely the opinion of the author. The author and publisher do not take any responsibility for any consequences that may result due to following the instructions provided in this book.

ISBN: 978-1530924349

Printed in the United States

Avant Propos

The weekend is coming up, and you are longing for a dish from your favorite French bistro. You think about making a reservation, but you realize this is becoming quite a habit. Maybe you should try to make your own French dishes at home...but, you think to yourself, there is no way you could recreate such flavors in your own kitchen.

Whether a meal in a French Bistro is a weekly occurrence or a special occasion treat is not going matter to you anymore! The true flavors of French Bistro cooking are found within this book and are accessible to everyone, from the novice who likes to experiment in the kitchen, to the seasoned cook who has attempted — and succeeded — at practically every style of cooking.

The recipes in this book are authentic to the various regions of France, bringing into your kitchen flavors that are ripe with the essence of the culture. From rustic chicken dishes to elegant duck, along with regional seafood and desserts that will kiss your soul, this book is a French bistro menu in and of itself. The next time you reach for the phone to make a reservation, try reaching for this book instead, and bring the flavors of Paris, Champagne, Lorraine, the Loire Valley, Burgundy, Bordeaux, Provence, or Normandy cooking into your own kitchen.

Bon appétit!

Contents

Introduction

What is French bistro cooking? Take a moment, and picture in your mind an intimate table, surrounded by those whose company you enjoy the most. You are talking, sharing stories and laughter while glasses of French wine dress your table like delicate jewels. In front you is placed a dish that compares to no other. The aroma is rustic and delicious, with flavors that come from nature and are made into something that is both subtle and magnificent at the same time. This is the essence of French bistro cooking.

The dishes that you find in a French bistro take the classic preparations of French cooking, combine them with ingredients that are native to the various regions of France, and elevate them to a dish that is simply unforgettable. Some of those dishes will be delicious in their simplicity and the way the natural flavors shine without effort, while other dishes are created to amaze and bless the palate with richness and velvetiness of sauces that were never before even imagined. If this sounds like a meal from a fairy tale to you, then you are not far off. There is something about the spirit of French cooking that is purely magical.

When thinking of French cooking, it is important to remember that the country of France is made up of many regions, each with its own pantry of ingredients and styles of preparation. This means that within French cooking, you will find an incredible variety of styles of dishes, from those that are simple in preparation and flavor, to those are a labor of love and decadent. In this

1

book, an effort has been made to present to you the finest and most loved of bistro-worthy dishes across many of these regions. The regions of Paris, Champagne, Lorraine, the Loire Valley, Burgundy, Bordeaux, Provence, and Normandy have all been represented in some way in the essence of these French Bistro dishes.

In order to taste the unique spirit of each of these regions in your cooking, it is vital that you use the best and freshest ingredients that are available to you in your area. This does not mean that you must spend a fortune to create an authentic French bistro dish. In fact, many dishes here are crafted with simple ingredients that are available at most grocery stores. The point is to honor the flavor of these ingredients by being choosy when it comes to selection. If you are making a specialty dish that contains duck or seafood, it is worth the effort to make a trip to your favorite meat or seafood market and ask the assistance of a professional in choosing the absolute best pieces for your dish. Free range and organic meats are superior choices for these dishes when they are available to you.

When it comes to the ingredients of French bistro cooking, you will find both variety and simplicity. Think in terms of fresh vegetables at their peak of ripeness, so much so that you can smell their flavor ready to burst from them. Rich and juicy meats that are silky and succulent when cooked, sweets that are a taste of heaven — and let's not forget about the regional staples; wine and cheese. You will find that many of the recipes in this book contain at least one, if not both of these ingredients. When wine is called for, use your favorite and always remember that if it is not worthy of sipping from a glass, then it is not worthy to be in your dish. When it comes to cheeses, classic, well known varieties have been used. If you are familiar with different French cheeses and would like to substitute a different cheese, then you should take the liberty of doing so. Just make sure that the cheese you choose is similar in texture and flavor to the original cheese used, if you wish to maintain the intended character of the dish.

Finally, when cooking these French-inspired dishes, keep in mind the spirit and passion of the region and infuse your own dishes with it as you cook. Anyone can throw ingredients together, but the spirit you put into your dishes is what makes the difference between good and fantastically authentic.

Bistro Appetizers

French Tapenade

Cook Time: none
Prep Time: 10 minutes
Serves: 8

Ingredients:
2 cups olives niçoises, or a dark olive
½ cup capers

¼ cup anchovy fillets
¼ cup shallots, chopped
1 tablespoon fresh thyme
1 teaspoon fresh oregano
1 tablespoon lemon juice
1 teaspoon lemon zest
1 teaspoon coarse ground black pepper
¼ cup extra virgin olive oil (approximate)
Crackers or toasted baguette slices for serving

Directions:

1. Begin by thoroughly rinsing the olives, capers, and anchovy fillets to remove excess salt.
2. Gently pat each dry and place in a blender or food processor.
3. Add the shallots, thyme oregano, lemon juice, lemon zest, and ground black pepper.
4. Blend or chop, slowly adding in the olive oil just until a spreadable paste forms. Use more or less olive oil depending upon personal preferences.
5. Remove from the blender or food processor and place in a serving bowl.
6. Serve with crackers or toasted baguette slices.

Millefeuille de Pelardons (Puff Pastry Stuffed with Goat Cheese Dressed with Provence Herbs)

Cook Time: 10 minutes
Prep Time: 15 minutes
Serves: 8-10

Ingredients:
1 puff pastry dough
2 round Pelardons goat cheeses or any semi-firm goat cheeses
1 tablespoon dry Provence herbs
Olive oil
Fresh cracked black pepper

Directions:
1. Preheat the oven to 375°F and line a baking sheet with parchment paper.

2. Roll the puff pastry dough out in a large rectangle. Cut in 8 equal squares.
3. Slice the goat cheese in 2 on the horizontal.
4. To assemble your puff pastry, place a goat cheese slice in the middle of a square of dough. Evenly add the Provence herbs on each piece of cheese with a bit of olive oil. Season with freshly cracked black pepper. Place a square of dough on top. Seal the edges by pressing.
5. Brush some of the egg wash on each pastry. Score each square with a diamond pattern. Bake in the oven for 30-40 minutes, or until the pastry is golden brown.
6. Serve immediately.

Fleurs de Courgettes Frites (Fried Zucchini Flowers)

Cook Time: 5 minutes
Prep Time: 20 minutes
Serves: 6

Ingredients:
12 zucchini flowers
½ cup sparkling water
¼ cup dry white wine
2 eggs, separated
1 teaspoon lemon zest
1 ½ cups all-purpose flour
1 teaspoon dried tarragon
1 teaspoon salt
1 teaspoon coarse ground black pepper
Vegetable oil for frying

Directions:

1. Place the egg yolks in a bowl and beat lightly with a whisk.
2. Add the sparkling water, white wine, and lemon zest. Whisk lightly.
3. In a separate bowl, mix together the all-purpose flour, tarragon, salt, and black pepper. Slowly add the flour to the egg mixture in several increments. Mix and let sit for 15-20 minutes.
4. While the mixture is sitting, beat the egg whites until stiff and set aside. Pour the oil in a deep skillet over medium-high heat.
5. Fold the egg whites into the batter.
6. Dip the zucchini flowers into the batter, letting any excess drip off before placing them into the hot oil.
7. Fry until golden, turning as needed to ensure even cooking, for 3-5 minutes.
8. Remove from the oil and allow to drain on a paper towel before serving.

Moules Marinières (Mussels with White Wine)

Cook Time: 15 minutes
Prep Time: 10 minutes
Serves: 6 as an appetizer

Ingredients:
2 pounds mussels, washed, with beards removed
¼ cup butter
4 cloves garlic, crushed and minced
½ cup dry white wine
2 teaspoons sherry vinegar
¼ cup fresh parsley, chopped
1 tablespoon fresh thyme, chopped
1 teaspoon cornstarch
½ teaspoon salt
1 teaspoon coarse ground black pepper

Directions:

1. Heat the butter in a deep skillet over medium heat.
2. Once the butter has melted, add the garlic and sauté until for 2 minutes.
3. Add the white wine, sherry vinegar, parsley, and thyme. Stir lightly until mixed.
4. Add the mussels to the skillet and increase the heat to medium-high. Bring the liquid to a boil and cook until the mussel shells open, approximately 5 minutes.
5. Remove the opened mussels and place them on a serving platter. Discard any mussels that have not opened.
6. Place the cornstarch in a small cup and add a bit of the cooking liquid. Whisk until a thin paste forms. Add the cornstarch paste to the cooking liquid and whisk gently.
7. Cook, while stirring, until the sauce thickens just slightly.
8. Season the sauce with salt and black pepper.
9. Pour the sauce over the mussels and serve immediately.

Spiced Duck Rillettes

Cook Time: 2 hours
Prep Time: 15 minutes plus approximately 24 hours for chilling
Serves: 8-10

Ingredients:
2 pounds duck legs
¼ cup coarse ground salt
1 tablespoon fresh ginger, grated
½ teaspoon ground cloves
1 tablespoon orange zest
2 tablespoons fresh thyme, chopped
8 cups duck stock
2 sprigs fresh rosemary
6 cloves garlic
2 star anise pods
1 tablespoon pink peppercorns
2 tablespoons Grand Marnier or orange flavored liqueur
⅔ cup duck fat, melted

Assorted toasts and crudités for serving
Additional rosemary sprigs for garnish, if desired

Directions:
1. In a bowl, combine the salt, ginger, cloves, orange zest, and thyme to create a rub.
2. Liberally pat the spice rub over the surface of the duck legs. Place the dug legs in a dish, cover, and refrigerate for 8-12 hours.
3. In a stock pot, combine the duck stock, rosemary, garlic, star anise, and pink peppercorns. Add the duck legs, and bring to a boil over medium-high heat.
4. Reduce the heat to medium-low, cover, and let simmer for 2 hours, or until the duck is fall-off-the-bone tender.
5. Turn off the heat, and let cool to room temperature before placing the entire stock pot in the refrigerator for 12 hours, or overnight.
6. Skim the fat off of the top of the stock, and remove the duck legs. Remove any skin and excess fat, and completely shred all of the duck meat. Discard the bones, and transfer the meat to a bowl.
7. Combine the duck meat with the orange liqueur and 1-2 tablespoons of the chilled duck stock from the stock pot.
8. Lay out four large serving ramekins, and firmly pack in the shredded duck meat. Press down until tightly compacted.
9. Melt the duck fat over low heat. Pour the melted duck fat into each of the ramekins. Cover tightly and chill for several hours, or until firm.

Mesclun Greens with Pear and Roquefort

Cook Time: none
Prep Time: 15 minutes
Serves: 6

Ingredients:
6 cups mesclun or a combination of arugula, dandelion greens, and endive
¼ cup fresh chervil, chopped
¼ cup extra virgin olive oil
1 tablespoon champagne vinegar
1 tablespoon shallots, diced
½ teaspoon salt
½ teaspoon black pepper
1 cup pear, sliced
¼ cup walnuts, chopped
½ cup Roquefort cheese, crumbled

Directions:

1. Combine the mesclun, or green mix, in a bowl with the chervil. Toss to mix.
2. In another bowl, combine the champagne vinegar and shallots. Slowly add the olive oil, whisking constantly, until well blended. Season with salt and black pepper.
3. Drizzle the dressing onto the salad greens and add the Roquefort cheese. Toss to mix, making sure the entire mixture is lightly coated with the dressing.
4. Place the mixture onto individual serving dishes, and garnish with slices of pear and some walnuts.
5. Serve immediately.

Soups and Stews

Potage Printanier (Green Spring Vegetable Soup)

Cook Time: 45 minutes
Prep Time: 10 minutes
Serves: 4-6

Ingredients:
1 tablespoon butter
2 cloves garlic, crushed and minced
½ cup leek, sliced
½ cup celery, diced
6 cups chicken or vegetable stock
1 cup turnip, chopped
1 cup white asparagus
1 cup fresh peas
¼ cup fresh parsley

1 tablespoon fresh tarragon, chopped
1 teaspoon salt
1 teaspoon black pepper
¼ cup crème fraiche
Pistachios, chopped, for garnish

Directions:

1. Melt the butter in a stock pot over medium heat.
2. Add the garlic, leek, and celery. Cook, stirring frequently, until the leeks begin to become tender, approximately 3 minutes.
3. Add the chicken or vegetable stock, increase the heat to medium-high and bring to a boil.
4. Add the turnips, white asparagus, and peas.
5. Cover, reduce heat to low, and let simmer for 30-40 minutes.
6. Strain the vegetables out of the stock and place them, along with ½ cup of the stock, in a blender or food processor. Blend until smooth.
7. Combine all of the cooking stock and pureed vegetables together in the stock pot.
8. Season with parsley, tarragon, salt, and black pepper. Cook over low heat for 5-10 minutes.
9. Ladle the soup into serving bowls and swirl a dollop of crème fraiche into the center of each bowl.
10. Serve immediately, garnished with chopped pistachios, if desired.

French Onion Soup

Cook Time: 40 minutes
Prep Time: 10 minutes
Serves: 4

Ingredients:
2 cups sweet yellow onion, sliced
½ cup sweet cream butter
½ teaspoon salt
1 tablespoon flour
4 cups beef stock
1 tablespoon fresh thyme
1 teaspoon coarse ground black pepper
4 baguette slices, approximately ½-inch thick
1 cup Gruyere cheese, shredded

Directions:
1. Melt the butter in a stock pot over medium heat.
2. Add the onions and salt, and sauté for 3 minutes. Add the flour and stir.

3. Add the beef stock, increase the heat to medium-high, and bring to a boil. Let boil for 1 minute.
4. Reduce the heat to low, season with thyme and black pepper. Cover and let simmer for 25-30 minutes.
5. While the soup is simmering, toast the baguette slices to a medium golden brown.
6. Preheat the broiler.
7. When the soup is done simmering, ladle it into oven proof serving bowls.
8. Top each bowl with a toasted baguette slice and shredded Gruyere cheese. Place under the broiler for 1-2 minutes, or until the cheese is melted and lightly caramelized.
9. Remove from the broiler carefully and serve immediately.

Armorican Fish Stew

Cook Time: 45 minutes
Prep Time: 15 minutes
Serves: 8-10

Ingredients:
¼ cup olive oil
½ pound crab meat
2 tablespoons brandy
½ cup bacon, diced
3 cloves garlic, crushed and minced
1 cup onion, diced
1 cup carrot, peeled and diced
1 cup celery, diced
½ cup leeks, sliced
2 cups tomatoes, diced
2 cups potatoes, peeled and diced
8 cups fish stock
2 bay leaves

1 tablespoon fresh thyme
1 tablespoon fresh oregano
1 teaspoon salt
1 teaspoon black pepper
2 teaspoons paprika
½ pound cod, cubed
12 scallops
½ pound mussels
Toasted baguette cubes for garnish

Directions:

1. Heat the olive oil over medium-high heat in a stock pot.
2. Add the crab meat and sauté for 2 minutes.
3. Add the brandy, and let it reduce for 2-3 minutes.
4. Remove the crab meat and set it aside.
5. Add the bacon and cook until lightly browned, approximately 3-5 minutes.
6. Add the garlic, onion, carrots, celery, and leeks. Sauté until slightly tender, approximately 5-7 minutes.
7. Add the tomatoes, potatoes, and fish stock. Bring to a boil for 1 minute before reducing heat to low.
8. Season with bay leaves, thyme, oregano, salt, black pepper, and paprika. Cover and simmer for 20 minutes.
9. Add the crab meat back in, together with the cod and scallops. Cook for an additional ten minutes, or until the cod and scallops are cooked through.
10. Add the mussels and simmer until the shells open.
11. Ladle into serving bowls, and garnish with toasted baguette cubes for serving.

La Potée Lorraine (Lorraine Stew)

Cook Time: 1 ½ hours
Prep Time: 15 minutes
Serves: 8-10

Ingredients:
2 tablespoons butter
2 tablespoons shallots, diced
1 cup carrots, diced
1 cup celery, diced
½ pound bacon, diced
1 pound pork roast, cubed
1 pound smoked sausage, sliced
1 ham bone
8 cups vegetable stock
2 teaspoons herbs de province
2 bay leaves
2 cups turnips, chopped
3 cups cabbage, sliced

Directions:
1. Place the butter in a stock pot and heat over medium.
2. Add the shallots and sauté until just tender, approximately 2 minutes.
3. Add the carrots and celery. Cook, stirring frequently for 4-5 minutes.
4. Add the bacon and cook until just browned, approximately 5 minutes.
5. Add the pork roast, sausage, ham bone, and vegetable stock. Increase the heat to medium-high and bring to a boil.

6. Reduce the heat to low, cover, and simmer for 1 hour.
7. Add the herbs de province, bay leaves, turnips, and cabbage.
8. Cover and continue to simmer for 30-45 minutes, or until the turnips are tender. Remove the ham bone and the bay leaves, and ladle the soup into serving bowls.
9. Serve warm.

Potato Leek Soup

Cook Time: 40 minutes
Prep Time: 10 minutes
Serves: 6-8

Ingredients:
4 tablespoons butter, divided
1 cup leeks, sliced
2 tablespoons shallots
¼ cup dry white wine
4 cups red potatoes, peeled and diced
8 cups chicken stock
1 sprig fresh rosemary
1 tablespoon fresh tarragon
1 teaspoon salt
1 teaspoon coarse ground black pepper
½ cup heavy cream

Directions:
1. Heat the butter in a stock pot over medium heat.
2. Add the leeks and shallots. Sauté, stirring frequently, for 4-5 minutes.
3. Add the white wine and let it reduce for 2 minutes.
4. Add the chicken stock, potatoes, rosemary, tarragon, salt, and black pepper.
5. Increase heat to medium-high and bring to a low boil.
6. Reduce the heat to low, cover, and simmer for 25-30 minutes, or until potatoes are tender.
7. With a hand held blender, purée the soup leaving some potato chunks for added texture.
8. Add cream and mix well and heat through before serving.

Cream of Watercress Soup

Cook Time: 30 minutes
Prep Time: 10 minutes
Serves: 6-8

Ingredients:
2 tablespoons butter
2 tablespoons shallots
¼ cup dry white wine
3 cups potatoes, peeled and cubed
2 cups watercress, chopped
6 cups chicken stock
½ cup crème fraiche
½ teaspoon nutmeg
1 teaspoon salt
1 teaspoon black pepper

Directions:
1. Heat the butter in a stock pot and over medium heat, and sauté the shallots for 2-3 minutes.
2. Add the dry white wine, and let it reduce for 2 minutes.
3. Add the potatoes, watercress, and chicken stock. Increase the heat to medium-high and bring to a boil.
4. Reduce the heat to low, cover, and let simmer for 20 minutes.
5. Transfer the soup to a blender and puree. Add the pureed soup back into the stock pot.
6. Add the crème fraiche and season with nutmeg, salt, and black pepper. Mix well and heat through before serving.

Classic Chicken and Poultry

Cassoulet

Cook Time: 4-6 hours
Prep Time: 20 minutes
Serves: 6-8

Ingredients:
1 pound bone-in chicken pieces
2 duck legs confit
1 pound chicken or pork sausage in casing, sliced

2 cups dried white beans, soaked for 12 hours in water and drained
½ pound pork skins
1 ham bone
1 cup onion, diced
1 cup carrot, diced
1 cup celery, diced
8 cloves garlic
2 bay leaves
1 tablespoon fresh thyme
1 sprig fresh rosemary
1 spring fresh sage
1 teaspoon salt
1 teaspoon coarse ground black pepper
Water

Directions:

1. Place some water in a large saucepan over medium-high heat and bring to a boil.
2. Add the beans to the saucepan and blanch for 3-5 minutes. Remove the beans from the pan to a strainer. Rinse lightly with cool water, and drain.
3. Add the beans to a large, deep, cast iron skillet or Dutch oven. Stir in the pork skins, ham bone, onion, carrots, celery, garlic, and enough water to cover all of the ingredients by about an inch.
4. Bring the liquid to a boil over medium-high heat before reducing the heat to low, covering, and simmering for 1 hour.
5. After 1 hour, remove the pork skins and the garlic cloves. Chop both of them into fine pieces and sauté in a dry skillet for 3-5 minutes. Transfer the mixture to a blender or food processor and puree before adding back into the skillet or Dutch oven.

6. Once again, add enough water to the skillet or Dutch oven to completely cover the ingredients. Replace the cover and simmer for an additional hour.
7. Preheat the oven to 375°F.
8. Once the ingredients have simmered for the additional hour add the chicken, duck confit and chicken or pork sausage.
9. Take the bay leaves, thyme, rosemary, and sage and tie them up together in a small piece of cheesecloth. Place the cheesecloth in the skillet with the meat.
10. Add enough water to cover the ingredients and place it in the oven. Check after 1 hour and add more water to replace that which has evaporated.
11. Repeat checking and refilling with water once an hour until the casserole has formed a caramelized, fragrant crust and the meat is completely cooked through. This may take from 3 to 6 hours, depending upon the size of the skillet or Dutch oven used.

Poule au Pot (Sunday Pot Chicken)

Cook Time: 3 hours
Prep Time: 20 minutes
Serves: 6-8

Ingredients:

1 3-4 pound whole chicken, innards removed
1 tablespoon olive oil
1 cup pancetta, diced
1 cup yellow onion, diced
1 chicken liver, chopped
2 cups white bread crumbs
1 egg, lightly beaten
1 teaspoon rubbed sage
1 teaspoon salt
1 teaspoon black pepper
½ pound carrots, cut into chunks
2 leeks
2 cups fennel bulb, sliced thick
6 cloves garlic
6 cups chicken stock
1 sprig fresh rosemary

Directions:

1. Place the olive oil in a sauté pan over medium heat. Add the pancetta, onion, and chicken liver, and cook until the pancetta is slightly crisp, approximately 5-6 minutes. Remove and set aside to cool slightly.
2. In a large bowl, combine the bread crumbs, egg, sage, salt, and black pepper. Toss to mix. Add the pancetta mixture and mix well.

3. Lay out a large piece of cheesecloth and place the mixture in the center of it. Tie the cheesecloth together with a piece of twine.
4. In a Dutch oven that is large enough to hold the chicken, bring the chicken stock to a boil over medium-high heat.
5. Place the pouch of stuffing into the center cavity of the chicken and place the chicken in the pot.
6. Using kitchen twine, pull the chicken legs up and tie the chicken tightly.
7. Place the carrots, leeks, fennel, garlic and rosemary in the pot surrounding the chicken.
8. Reduce the heat to low or medium-low and cook, with the stock bubbling gently, for approximately 2 ½ hours or until chicken is cooked through.
9. Preheat the oven to 350°F.
10. Remove the chicken from the pot and set it on a board to rest. Remove the pouch of stuffing, open it up and transfer the stuffing to a baking dish.
11. Place the baking dish in the oven and bake for 15 minutes or until the temperature of the stuffing measures 160°F on a kitchen thermometer.
12. Transfer the chicken to a serving platter along with the stuffing and vegetables for serving.

Canard à la Moutarde (Duck with Mustard Sauce)

Cook Time: 50 minutes
Prep Time: 10 minutes
Serves: 4-6

:

1 whole duck, cut into pieces
1 teaspoon salt
1 teaspoon coarse ground black pepper
⅔ cup high quality Dijon mustard
¼ cup butter, divided
2 tablespoons shallots, chopped
½ cup dry white wine
1 sprig fresh rosemary
1 tablespoon fresh thyme, chopped
1 teaspoon ground sage
½ cup crème fraiche

Directions:

1. Season the duck liberally with salt and black pepper and then brush each piece completely with the Dijon mustard.
2. Heat 1 tablespoon of the butter in a large skillet over medium-high heat. Add the duck pieces and sear on all sides. Continue to cook until the skin of the duck just begins to caramelize and become slightly crispy, approximately 10-12 minutes. Remove it from the pan and set it aside.
3. Add the remaining 3 tablespoons of butter to the pan to melt.
4. Add the shallots and cook for 2-3 minutes, or until the shallots are tender.
5. Add the white wine and stir, scraping up the crispy bits along the bottom of the pan as the wine reduces slightly, for 1-2 minutes.
6. Reduce the heat of the pan to medium, and place the duck back into the pan.
7. Season with rosemary, thyme, and sage. Cover and cook for approximately 30 minutes, or until the duck is cooked through and tender.
8. Remove the duck from the pan and transfer to a serving platter.
9. Add the crème fraiche to the pan and stir until blended. Pour the pan sauce over the duck and serve immediately.

Chicken Fricassee with Tarragon Cream Sauce

Cook Time: 40 minutes
Prep Time: 10 minutes
Serves: 6

Ingredients:

2 pounds bone-in chicken pieces
¼ cup butter, divided
1 teaspoon salt, divided
1 teaspoon coarse ground black pepper
½ teaspoon garlic powder
1 cup dry white wine
2 cups chicken stock
1 cup cipolinni onions
2 cups white asparagus, chopped
2 cups mushrooms, sliced thick
1 teaspoon white sugar
2 cups crème fraiche
1 tablespoon fresh tarragon
1 teaspoon lemon zest

Directions:

1. Place 2 tablespoons of the butter in a large skillet or Dutch oven over medium-high heat.
2. Season the chicken with black pepper, garlic powder, and half a teaspoon of the salt.
3. Place the chicken in the skillet and brown, approximately 2 minutes per side.

4. Add the dry white wine and chicken stock. Bring to a low boil before reducing the heat, covering and simmering for 20-25 minutes, or until the chicken pieces are cooked through.
5. Add the remaining butter to a large sauté pan over medium heat.
6. Add the cipolinni onions and asparagus. Saute for 3-5 minutes.
7. Add the mushrooms, sugar, and remaining salt. Sauté for an additional 2-3 minutes, or until the mushrooms are tender. Set aside.
8. When the chicken has finished cooking, remove it from the pan and keep it warm.
9. Increase the heat of the skillet and reduce the sauce until it thickens slightly and has decreased in volume by about half.
10. Add the crème fraiche, tarragon, and lemon zest. Continue to cook, stirring frequently, until the sauce has reduced and thickened slightly, approximately 5 minutes.
11. Spoon the sautéed vegetables onto a serving platter, followed by the chicken and then the tarragon cream sauce for serving.

Duck Confit

Cook Time: 12 hours
Prep Time: 15 minutes plus 12 hours chilling time
Serves: 6-8

Ingredients:
2 ½ pounds duck legs
2 tablespoons coarse ground salt, divided
1 teaspoon coarse ground black pepper
6 cloves garlic
2 sprigs fresh rosemary
1 sprig fresh thyme
4 ½ cups high quality olive oil

Directions:
1. Remove any excess fat from the duck legs and reserve.
2. Season the meat with 1 tablespoon of the salt and the black pepper.

3. Divide the duck legs into two portions. Use the reserved duck fat to line the bottom of a lidded container (preferably glass).
4. Lay the first portion of duck skin side down in the container on top of the duck fat.
5. Place the garlic, rosemary, and thyme on top of the first layer of duck.
6. Follow with the remaining pieces of duck, placed with their skin side up, and sprinkle the remaining salt on top.
7. Cover and refrigerate for 12-16 hours.
8. Preheat the oven to a low 225°F.
9. Remove the duck from the container and brush off any excess visible salt.
10. Place the duck in a heavy, oven proof casserole dish, along with the spices and fat that were used during refrigeration.
11. Add the olive oil to the pan. Cover and place in the oven to bake for 10-12 hours, or until the duck is fall-off-the-bone tender.
12. Remove the duck from the pan, reserving the fat it was cooked in.
13. Pull the meat from the duck bones and place it in a container.
14. Cover the duck meat with the reserved cooking fat and store in the refrigerator until ready to serve or use in another dish.

Coq Au Vin

Cook Time: 1 hour
Prep Time: 15 minutes
Serves: 6-8

Ingredients:
2 tablespoons olive oil
1 cup pancetta, chopped
2 pounds bone-in chicken pieces
1 teaspoon salt
1 teaspoon black pepper
3 cups carrots, peeled and sliced
1 cup yellow onion, sliced
1 cup turnip, chopped
2 cups mushrooms, quartered
2 tablespoons shallots, diced
½ cup brandy
3 cups dry red wine
1 cup chicken stock

1 tablespoon fresh thyme, chopped
1 tablespoon fresh oregano, chopped
1 sprig fresh rosemary
2 tablespoons sweet cream butter, melted
1 tablespoon flour

Directions:
1. Heat the olive oil in a Dutch oven over medium heat.
2. Add the pancetta and cook, stirring frequently, until browned, approximately 5 minutes.
3. Remove the pancetta with a slotted spoon and set aside.
4. Season the chicken with salt and pepper and then place the chicken in the Dutch oven and cook until browned, approximately 3-5 minutes per side. Remove the chicken and set aside.
5. Add the carrots, onion, and turnip to the Dutch oven. Cook, stirring frequently for 5-7 minutes.
6. Add the mushrooms and shallots. Cook for 2-3 minutes.
7. Place the chicken and pancetta back into the Dutch oven.
8. Add the brandy, red wine, and chicken stock. Season with the thyme, oregano and rosemary.
9. Increase the heat to medium-high until the liquid just begins to bubble. Reduce the heat to low, cover, and simmer for 35-40 minutes.
10. Combine the butter and flour and stir it into the liquid of the Dutch oven. Cover and cook for an additional 10-15 minutes.
11. Remove from heat and let rest 10 minutes before serving.

Duck Breast in Sweet Lavender Sauce

Cook Time: 20 minutes
Prep Time: 10 minutes
Serves: 4-6

Ingredients:

4 duck breasts
½ teaspoon salt
1 teaspoon coarse ground black pepper
2 tablespoons lavender honey
2 tablespoons shallots, diced
½ cup sweet white wine
2 cups homemade duck or chicken stock
2 teaspoons fresh thyme
1 sprig fresh rosemary
1 teaspoon dried lavender flowers, finely crushed
1 tablespoon sweet cream butter

Directions:

1. Preheat the oven to 375°F.
2. Liberally brush the skin sides of the duck breasts with lavender honey and season with salt and black pepper.
3. Heat an oven proof skillet over medium heat and add the duck breasts, skin side down. Brown the duck on both sides until lightly caramelized.
4. Transfer the skillet to the oven and bake for 7-10 minutes, or until the inside reaches a warm pink, and reaches 160°F.
5. Remove the duck from the pan and let rest.
6. Add the shallots to the pan over medium heat. Cook, stirring gently, until the shallots just begin to caramelize, approximately 3-5 minutes.

7. Add the white wine and let it reduce for 2 minutes, stirring frequently.
8. Add the duck or chicken stock, thyme, rosemary, and lavender flowers. Cook, stirring frequently over medium-high heat, until the sauce has reduced and thickened slightly.
9. Remove from the heat and stir in the butter.
10. Slice the duck breasts into thin pieces and arrange them on a serving platter.
11. Drizzle the sauce over the duck right before serving.

Delectable Pork and Veal Dishes

Veal Medallions with Morels

Cook Time: 2 ½ hours
Prep Time: 15 minutes
Serves: 6-8

Ingredients:
1 ½ pound boneless veal roast
2 tablespoons butter
2 tablespoons shallots, diced
2 cups morel mushrooms, chopped
½ cup crème fraiche
½ cup goat cheese
2 tablespoons fresh thyme, chopped, divided
1 teaspoon salt
1 teaspoon black pepper
½ pound bacon
2 cups carrots, chopped
1 cup red potatoes, cubed
1 cup turnips, chopped
4 cups chicken stock
½ cup dry white wine
1 sprig fresh rosemary

Directions:
1. Slice the veal in half 2/3 of the way through and open up as in a butterfly cut. Using a meat mallet, flatten the veal slightly.
2. Heat the butter in a large cast iron skillet or Dutch oven over medium heat.

3. Add the shallots and mushrooms and sauté just until tender, approximately 2-3 minutes. Using a slotted spoon, remove the mushrooms and shallots from the pan and set aside.
4. In a bowl, combine the crème fraiche, goat cheese, 1 tablespoon of the thyme, and the shallots and mushrooms. Mix well.
5. Season the veal with salt and black pepper. Spread the cream mixture onto the top side of the veal.
6. Roll the veal up and secure with kitchen twine. Place the veal into the pan, along with the bacon, and brown evenly on all sides.
7. Place the carrots, potatoes, and turnips in the pan, followed by the chicken stock and white wine.
8. Increase the heat to medium-high and bring the liquid to a low boil.
9. Reduce the heat, season with the remaining thyme and rosemary, cover, and let simmer for up to 2 hours, or until the meat is cooked through.
10. Remove the meat and vegetables from the pan and set aside to rest.
11. Increase the heat to medium-high and reduce the pan sauce by about half.
12. Remove the twine from the veal and slice into 1-inch medallions.
13. Place on a serving plate with the vegetables and drizzle with the pan gravy before serving.

Tourte Lorraine (Lorraine Pie)

Cook Time: 1 hour 20 minutes
Prep Time: 15 minutes plus marinating time
Serves: 6

Ingredients:

½ pound veal, sliced thin
½ pound smoked ham, sliced into strips
2 cups dry white wine
1 sprig rosemary
4 cloves garlic
2 sheets puff pastry
2 cups red potatoes, finely chopped
1 cup mushrooms, sliced
2 eggs, lightly beaten
½ cup goat cheese
2 cups crème fraiche

Directions:

1. Place the veal and ham slices in a together bowl, with the rosemary and garlic cloves. Add the white wine, cover, and let marinate for 12-24 hours.
2. Preheat the oven to 350°F.
3. Cut out circles from the two sheets of puff pastry to fit into a deep pie dish or spring form pan. In one of the sheets of the puff pastry, cut a 1-2 inch hole in the center.
4. Place the puff pastry without the hole in the bottom of the deep dish pie pan.
5. Place the marinated meat, potatoes and mushrooms into the pan.

6. Cover with the puff pastry with a hole in the center.
7. Place in the oven and bake for 45 minutes.
8. Combine the eggs, goat cheese, and crème fraiche. Mix until creamy.
9. Remove the pie from the oven and pour the egg mixture into the center hole of the top crust.
10. Place the pie back into the oven and bake for an additional 35 minutes, or until set.
11. Serve warm.

Croque Monsieur

Cook Time: 15 minutes
Prep Time: 10 minutes
Serves: 4

Ingredients:
2 tablespoons butter
2 tablespoons flour
1 ½ cups milk, heated
3 cups Gruyere cheese, divided
1 teaspoon salt
1 teaspoon coarse ground black pepper
½ teaspoon nutmeg
8 slices thick white bread, crusts trimmed, toasted
1 tablespoon champagne mustard
½ pound smoked ham, sliced thin
½ cup Brie cheese, slice
1 tablespoon fresh chives, chopped

Directions:

1. Preheat the oven to 400°F. Line a baking sheet with parchment paper.
2. In a saucepan, heat the butter over medium heat. Sprinkle in the flour and whisk until a paste forms.
3. Slowly add the warm milk, whisking constantly until creamy. Season with salt, pepper, and nutmeg. Continue cooking, stirring constantly, until the sauce thickens.
4. Remove from the heat and add 2 cups of Gruyere cheese.
5. On each piece of bread, spread a little champagne mustard and then make sandwiches with a layer of ham and brie cheese.
6. Coat each of the sandwiches with the cream sauce on both sides. With a spatula, transfer the sandwiches to the baking sheet. Sprinkle the sandwiches with half of the remaining Gruyere cheese.
7. Place the sandwiches in the oven and bake for 7 minutes. Remove from the oven and turn over using a spatula.
8. Sprinkle the remaining Gruyere cheese on the sandwiches and bake for an additional 5 minutes.
9. Turn the broiler on high, and place the sandwiches under it until they are golden and crispy, approximately 1-2 minutes.
10. Remove from the oven and serve immediately, garnished with fresh chives.

Pancetta and Shallot Pie

Cook Time: 50 minutes
Prep Time: 15 minutes
Serves: 6

Ingredients:
¼ teaspoon dry yeast
5 cups plus one tablespoon all-purpose flour
1 tablespoon salt
1 cup water
2 cups pancetta, diced
3 tablespoons shallots, diced
2 cups cottage cheese or farmer's cheese
½ cup crème fraiche
1 teaspoon nutmeg
1 teaspoon black pepper

Directions:
1. Combine the yeast with 2 tablespoons of warm water and mix. Set aside for 30 minutes.
2. Sift 5 cups of flour and the salt into a mound on the counter. Form a well in the center of the mound.
3. Add the yeast mixture to the center of the well. Begin working the dough inward from the outside, adding water as you go to keep the dough at a workable consistency.
4. Knead the dough for 10 minutes, form it into a ball, cover and set it aside for 30 minutes.
5. Preheat the oven to 400°F.
6. Place the pancetta in a skillet over medium heat, and sauté until browned, approximately 5-7

minutes. Add the shallots and cook until tender, approximately 3-5 minutes.

7. Roll out the pastry dough to line a deep pie dish, and another piece to cover it.

8. Combine the cottage cheese, crème fraiche, remaining tablespoon of flour, nutmeg, and black pepper. Mix until creamy.

9. Place the bottom pastry into the deep pie dish, and the spread with the cheese mixture. Place the pancetta mixture in a layer on top of the cheese.

10. Cover with the remaining piece of dough and trim along the edges.

11. Place in the oven and bake until golden, approximately 35-40 minutes.

12. Serve warm.

Porte Maillot Ham

Cook Time: 4 hours
Prep Time: 15 minutes
Serves: 8-10

Ingredients:
1 5-pound bone-in ham
2 cups onions, sliced
2 cups carrots, chopped
6 cloves garlic
1 tablespoon fresh thyme, chopped
1 teaspoon cloves
2 bay leaves
½ teaspoon cinnamon
½ teaspoon nutmeg
Water
1 tablespoon butter
3 tablespoons shallots, diced
1 ½ cups dry white wine
2 cups beef stock
¼ cup fresh parsley, chopped

Directions:
1. Score the surface of the ham in a diagonal pattern and wrap it up tightly in a large piece of cheesecloth.
2. Place the ham into a Dutch oven, together with the onions, carrots, and garlic.
3. Add enough water to just cover the ham, and season with thyme, cloves, bay leaves, cinnamon, and nutmeg.

4. Bring the liquid to a gentle boil. Reduce the heat to medium-low, cover and simmer for 3 ½ to 4 hours.
5. Remove the ham and the vegetables from the Dutch oven and discard the liquid.
6. Carefully peel the cheesecloth from the ham, and remove the meat from the bone. Place the meat and the vegetables back into the pot.
7. Heat the butter in a large skillet over medium-high heat.
8. Add the shallots and sauté until just tender, approximately 3 minutes.
9. Add the white wine and reduce for 2 minutes before adding the beef stock and parsley.
10. Cook over medium-high heat and reduce slightly.
11. Pour the sauce over the ham, cover and simmer for 30 minutes.
12. Serve warm.

Ham, Cheese and Apple Tart

Cook Time: 45 minutes
Prep Time: 15 minutes plus chilling time
Serves: 6

Ingredients:
2 cups all-purpose flour
1 teaspoon salt
1 cup chilled butter, diced
1 egg yolk
¼ cup water
3 eggs, lightly beaten
¼ cup crème fraiche
½ cup goat cheese
1 cup Gouda cheese, shredded
2 cups smoked ham, diced
2 cups apples, diced
1 tablespoon shallots, diced
½ teaspoon nutmeg
1 teaspoon coarse ground black pepper

Directions:
1. Sift the flour and salt into a mound on a countertop.
2. Make a well in the center of the flour and add the butter and egg yolk. Work the dough with your hands, gradually adding the water until a firm dough forms.
3. Form the dough into a ball, cover and refrigerate for 2 hours.
4. Preheat the oven to 400°F.
5. Butter and flour a spring form or tart pan.
6. Roll out the dough into a thin layer and use it to line the bottom of the pan.
7. In a bowl, combine the eggs and crème fraiche until creamy. Add the goat cheese and Gouda. Blend well.
8. Stir in the ham, apples, and shallots. Season with nutmeg and black pepper.
9. Pour the mixture over the crust in the pan.
10. Place the tart in the oven and bake for 5 minutes.
11. Reduce the heat to 350°F and continue baking for 35-40 minutes or until golden brown and set.
12. Serve warm.

French Beef Masterpieces

Provençale Beef

Cook Time: 50 minutes
Prep Time: 10 minutes the marinade time
Serves: 6

Ingredients:

2 pounds beef roast, cubed

¼ cup olive oil, divided

4 cups dry red wine

1 sprig rosemary

1 cup pancetta, diced

2 cups carrots, peeled and chopped

2 cups sweet yellow onion, sliced

2 cups mushrooms, quartered

1 cup celery, chopped

2 cups tomatoes, diced

1 cup black olives, halved

2 cups beef stock
1 tablespoon fresh thyme, chopped
1 tablespoon fresh oregano, chopped
½ teaspoon rubbed sage
1 teaspoon salt
1 teaspoon black pepper
1 tablespoon orange zest

Directions:

1. Combine three tablespoons of the olive oil, red wine, and rosemary in a large bowl. Add the cubed beef pieces, cover, and marinade for 12-24 hours.
2. Preheat the oven to 375°F.
3. Pour the remaining olive oil in a large, deep, oven proof skillet over medium heat.
4. Remove the beef from the marinade and place it in the skillet, together with the pancetta. Cook until lightly browned, approximately 5-7 minutes.
5. Add the carrots, onion, mushroom, celery, tomatoes, and black olives.
6. Add the beef stock, along with 2 cups of the used marinade to the skillet.
7. Season with thyme, oregano, sage, salt, black pepper, and orange zest.
8. Cover and place in the oven. Bake for approximately 45 minutes, or until the meat is cooked through and tender.

Beef with Poulette Sauce

Cook Time: 20 minutes
Prep Time: 10 minutes
Serves: 6

Ingredients:

2 pounds beef medallions
1 teaspoon salt
1 tablespoon black peppercorns
1 tablespoon butter
½ cup dry red wine
1 tablespoon duck fat
1 tablespoon flour
12 cups beef stock
½ cup crème fraiche
2 egg yolks, lightly beaten
1 tablespoon lemon juice
1 teaspoon lemon zest
½ teaspoon nutmeg
¼ cup fresh parsley

Directions:

1. Season the beef medallions with salt.
2. Heat the butter and peppercorns in a large skillet over medium heat.
3. Add the medallions and cook until browned, but still slightly pink in the center.
4. Add the red wine and let it reduce for 3 minutes.
5. Remove the medallions to a plate, cover, and keep warm.

6. Add the duck fat to the skillet and let it melt. Slowly whisk in the flour until a paste has formed. Continue to cook, stirring frequently to avoid burning, for approximately 3-5 minutes.
7. Slowly add the beef stock, whisking constantly, until it is completely incorporated.
8. In a bowl, combine the crème fraiche, egg yolk, lemon juice, lemon zest, and nutmeg. Mix well.
9. Add a small amount of the stock to the mixture and whisk quickly to temper the eggs.
10. Add the entire egg mixture into the pan with the stock, whisking briskly, and remove the pan from the heat.
11. Whisk until sauce has thickened and then place the beef medallions back into the sauce.
12. Serve immediately, garnished with fresh parsley.

Beef Bourguignon

Cook Time: 1 ½ hours
Prep Time: 10 minutes
Serves: 6-8

Ingredients:
2 pounds beef roast, cubed
½ pound pancetta, cubed
1 teaspoon salt
1 teaspoon coarse ground black pepper
½ teaspoon onion powder
½ teaspoon paprika
2 tablespoons flour
1 tablespoon olive oil
2 cups pearl onions
3 cups carrots, peeled and sliced
3 cups mushrooms, sliced
4 cloves garlic, crushed and minced
4 cups dry red wine

61

2 cups homemade beef stock
1 tablespoon tomato paste
1 sprig fresh rosemary
1 sprig fresh thyme
1 bay leaf

Directions:

1. Preheat the oven to 325°F
2. Place the pancetta in a Dutch oven or large oven proof skillet and heat over medium. Cook until the pancetta is nicely browned, approximately 5 minutes.
3. Season the beef with salt, black pepper, onion powder, and paprika and sprinkle lightly with the flour.
4. Add the beef to the skillet and cook until browned on all sides, approximately 5 minutes.
5. Remove the beef and pancetta from the skillet and add the olive oil to the pan.
6. Add the onions and carrots. Cook, stirring frequently, for 5 minutes. Add the mushrooms and garlic. Cook, while stirring, for 2 minutes.
7. Add the beef and pancetta back into the pan, along with the red wine and beef stock. Stir in the tomato paste.
8. Using kitchen twine, tie together the rosemary, thyme, and bay leaf and place them in the pot.
9. Bring the liquid to a boil before removing from the burner, covering, and placing in the oven.
10. Bake for 1 hour, or until the meat is cooked through and tender.
11. Let rest 10 minutes before serving.

Stuffed Steak with Red Wine Sauce

Cook Time: 40 minutes
Prep Time: 15 minutes
Serves: 4

Ingredients:
4 beef steaks, approximately 4-6 ounces each
1 teaspoon salt
1 teaspoon black pepper
¼ cup butter, divided
1 cup carrot, peeled and diced
½ cup celery, diced
1 tablespoon shallots, diced
2 cups fresh spinach, torn
½ cup Gruyere cheese, shredded
1 sprig fresh rosemary
1 tablespoon black peppercorns
2 cups dry red wine

Directions:
1. Preheat the oven to 375°F.
2. Season the steak with salt and black pepper. Along one side of each steak make a cut that goes approximately ¾ of the way through, to form a pocket.
3. Place one tablespoon of the butter into an oven proof skillet over medium heat.
4. Add the carrot, celery, and shallots. Cook, stirring frequently, for 5 minutes.
5. Add the spinach and cook an additional 2 minutes. Remove the vegetable mixture from the skillet, stir in the Gruyere cheese and set aside to cool slightly.

6. Place equal amounts of the mixture into the cut pouches of each steak.
7. Place the steaks in the pan, adding more butter if necessary, and brown on both sides, approximately 3 minutes per side.
8. Place the skillet in the oven and bake for approximately 30-35 minutes, or until the meat has reached your desired temperature.
9. Remove the steaks from the skillet and set aside to rest. Place the steaks under an aluminum foil tent to keep them warm.
10. Add the remaining butter, rosemary and peppercorns to the pan over medium-high heat.
11. Add the red wine and cook, stirring frequently, for 3 minutes as the wine reduces.
12. Reduce the heat to low and let the sauce simmer for 15 minutes.
13. Place the steaks on serving plates, drizzled with the red wine sauce for serving.

Coastal Seafood Creations

Mussels with Cream Sauce

Cook Time: 15 minutes
Prep Time: 10 minutes
Serves: 4

Ingredients:

2 pounds mussels, washed
3 tablespoons butter
1 cup leeks, sliced
1 tablespoon shallots, diced
¼ cup fresh parsley, chopped
1 ½ cups dry white wine
1 cup vegetable stock
¼ cup crème fraiche
1 teaspoon lemon zest
2 teaspoons fresh tarragon
½ teaspoon salt
½ teaspoon black pepper

Directions:

1. Place the butter in a large pot over medium-high heat.
2. Add the leeks and shallots, and sauté for 3 minutes.
3. Add the mussels, parsley, and white wine. Cook for 1 minute before adding the vegetable stock. Bring to a gentle boil.
4. Cook until the mussels open. Remove the mussels from the pan, and discard any that have not opened.
5. Remove the pot from the heat and add the crème fraiche, lemon zest, tarragon, salt, and black pepper. Whisk quickly until well blended.
6. Spoon the cream sauce into serving dishes and top with the mussels. Serve immediately.

Huitres Chaudes (Seared Oysters)

Cook Time: 10 minutes
Prep Time: 10 minutes
Serves: 4

Ingredients:
20 oysters in the shell
2 tablespoons butter
2 tablespoons shallots, diced
¼ cup dry white wine
1 cup fish stock
1 tablespoon lemon juice
½ teaspoon salt
1 teaspoon black pepper
½ cup crème fraiche

Directions:
1. Begin by opening the oysters and removing the top shell.
2. Place the butter in a saucepan and heat over medium-high.
3. Add the shallots and sauté for 2 minutes.
4. Add the white wine and reduce for 1 minute.
5. Add the fish stock, lemon juice, salt, and black pepper. Cook, stirring frequently while the sauce reduces by about half.
6. Add the crème fraiche and reduce the heat to medium. Continue to cook while the sauce reduces slightly more. Remove the pan from the heat.
7. Place the oysters open side up on a broiler pan. Place under the broiler for 1-2 minutes or until the oyster are just browned.

8. Spoon the sauce into serving dishes and carefully place the oyster shells on top.
9. Serve immediately.

Salmon with Butter Sauce

Cook Time: 25 minutes
Prep Time: 10 minutes
Serves: 4

Ingredients:
4 salmon fillets, approximately 4-6 ounces each
2 teaspoons olive oil
1 teaspoon salt
1 teaspoon black pepper
½ cup butter, cubed, divided
2 tablespoons shallots, diced
¼ cup champagne vinegar
¼ cup semi sweet white wine
1 tablespoon capers, rinsed
1 tablespoon fresh rosemary chopped (or 1 teaspoon dry rosemary)

Directions:

1. Preheat the oven to 350°F and line a baking sheet with parchment paper.
2. Brush both sides of the salmon with olive oil, and season with salt and black pepper.
3. Place the salmon fillets on the baking sheet and in the oven. Bake for 20-25 minutes, depending on the thickness of the fillets, until they are pink and flakey in the center.
4. Heat 1 tablespoon of the butter in a saucepan over medium heat.
5. Add the shallots and cook, while stirring, for 2 minutes.
6. Add the champagne vinegar and white wine. Continue to cook, while stirring, until most of the liquid has reduced, approximately 5 minutes.
7. Reduce the heat to medium-low and add the capers, rosemary, and the remaining butter in small increments, stirring constantly to avoid browning or burning, for 3-5 minutes.
8. Remove the pan from the heat.
9. Remove the salmon from the oven and arrange on serving plates. Drizzle the butter sauce lightly over the top and around the salmon before serving.

Sole Meunière

Cook Time: 15 minutes
Prep Time: 10 minutes
Serves: 4

Ingredients:
4 sole fillets, about 4 ounces each
½ cup all-purpose flour
3 tablespoons olive oil
3 tablespoons butter
½ teaspoon salt
Freshly ground pepper
Lemon wedges for serving

Sauce
½ cup unsalted butter
2 tablespoons fresh lemon juice
½ teaspoon lemon zest

¼ cup fresh parsley, chopped

Directions:
1. Rinse the fish fillets and pat dry with paper towels.
2. In a shallow dish, add the flour, salt and pepper. Stir to combine. Dredge each fillet with the seasoned flour on both side. Shake to remove the excess flour. Set aside.
3. Heat the olive oil and butter in a large heavy bottomed skillet over medium heat.
4. Add the sole fillets and cook for 3 minutes before turning over and cooking for 1-2 minutes more until the fish is cooked through and golden. Remove fish from skillet and loosely cover with foil to keep warm. Discard excess fat and drippings from the skillet.
5. To the skillet, add unsalted butter and let melt. Stir occasionally to free the bits and pieces from the bottom of the pan. Cook 1-2 minutes until the butter start bubbling and becoming golden. Add the lemon juice, zest, and parsley. Stir a few times to combine well. Remove from heat.
6. Place fillets on serving plates. Evenly add the sauce over each sole. Serve with lemon wedges.

Pike with Shallots

Cook Time: 30 minutes
Prep Time: 10 minutes
Serves: 4

Ingredients:
1 pound pike, cut into 4 pieces
1 teaspoon salt
1 teaspoon black pepper
2 tablespoons butter
3 tablespoons shallots, sliced
1 tablespoon fresh thyme
¼ cup semi sweet white wine
¼ cup fish stock
Cooked polenta for serving

Directions:
1. Season the pike with salt and black pepper.
2. Preheat the oven to 400°F.
3. Place the butter in an ovenproof skillet over medium heat.
4. Add the shallots and thyme. Cook for 3-4 minutes, or until the shallots start to become tender.
5. Add the pike and cook over medium heat for 3-5 minutes.
6. Place the skillet in the oven and bake for 15 minutes.
7. Add the white wine and fish stock and continue cooking for an additional 10-15 minutes, or until the fish is cooked through.
8. Remove from the oven and serve on a bed of creamy polenta.

Vegetables and Side Dishes

French Ratatouille

Cook Time: 1 hour
Prep Time: 30 minutes
Serves: 4-6

Ingredients:

¼ cup olive oil
1 cup sweet yellow onion, sliced thick
4 cups eggplant, cut into large cubes
4 cloves garlic, crushed and minced
4 cups zucchini, cubed
1 cup yellow bell pepper, cubed
½ cup celery, chopped
4 cups ripe tomatoes, blanched, peeled and quartered
1 teaspoon salt
1 teaspoon black pepper
1 tablespoon fresh thyme

1 tablespoon fresh tarragon
¼ cup fresh parsley, chopped
1 sprig fresh rosemary

Directions:
1. Slice all vegetables in similar sizes.
2. Preheat the oven to 350°F.
3. Place the olive oil in a large, deep, oven proof skillet and heat over medium.
4. Add the onions and sauté until just tender, approximately 3 minutes.
5. Add the eggplant and cook for 5 minutes.
6. Next add the garlic, zucchini, bell peppers, and celery. Cook, stirring occasionally, for 5 minutes.
7. Add the tomatoes, along with any juice that they have produced, to the skillet along with the salt, black pepper, fresh thyme, tarragon, parsley, and rosemary. Toss gently to mix.
8. Cover, and place the skillet in the oven for 45 minutes, or until the vegetables are tender and fragrant.
9. Serve warm or chilled.

Quiche Lorraine

Cook Time: 40 minutes
Prep Time: 15 minutes plus chilling time
Serves: 6

Ingredients:
1 ½ cups all-purpose flour
½ teaspoon salt
¼ cup plus 1 tablespoon chilled butter, cubed
1 tablespoon olive oil
4 eggs, divided
½ pound ham cooked, diced
1 French shallots, diced
1 cup Gruyere cheese, shredded
½ cup crème fraiche
¼ teaspoon nutmeg

½ teaspoon sea salt
½ teaspoon coarse ground black pepper

Directions:

1. Sift the flour and salt together into a mound on the countertop and make a well in the center.
2. Into the well, crack one egg and add the butter. Using your fingers, mix the flour into the center of the well and mix until a firm dough forms. If you find that the dough is a little dry, add water a few drops at a time until the correct consistency is reached.
3. Knead the dough and form it into a ball. Cover and place in the refrigerator for 2 hours.
4. Preheat the oven to 425°F and lightly oil a round cake pan or deep pie dish.
5. Roll the pastry into a circle large enough to fit into your baking dish and cover the sides. The dough should be thin.
6. Place the dough in the pan and trim any sides that hang over the edges.
7. Warm olive oil in a skillet over medium heat. Add the shallots and cook for 2-3 minutes, until tender and fragrant. Add the ham and continue cooking for 1-2 minutes. Remove the ham and shallots with a slotted spoon and spread them in the bottom of the crust.
8. In a bowl, combine the eggs and crème fraiche. Using a whisk, blend until creamy.
9. Fold in the Gruyere cheese and season with nutmeg, salt, and pepper.
10. Pour the egg mixture over the ham and shallots.
11. Place in the oven and bake for 30-35 minutes, or until set in the center.

Cheese Soufflé

Cook Time: 20 minutes
Prep Time: 10 minutes
Serves: 4

Ingredients:
2 tablespoons butter
2 tablespoons flour
½ cup milk, heated
1 cup Gruyere cheese, shredded
3 eggs, separated
½ teaspoon salt
1 teaspoon black pepper
1 teaspoon nutmeg

Directions:
1. Preheat the oven to 350°F and lightly oil 4 soufflé ramequins.

2. Melt the butter in a saucepan over medium heat. Add the flour slowly and whisk until a paste forms.
3. Add the milk slowly, whisking constantly.
4. Reduce the heat to low and keep warm, stirring frequently to prevent burning or sticking.
5. Place the egg whites in a bowl and beat until stiff. Set aside.
6. Lightly beat the egg yolks and add them to the cream sauce, together with the cheese. Mix gently until the cheese has melted. Season with salt, black pepper, and nutmeg.
7. Gently fold in the egg whites and carefully spoon the mixture into the soufflé cups.
8. Place in the oven and bake for approximately 15 minutes.
9. Carefully remove the soufflé cups from the oven and serve immediately.

Artichoke Soufflé

Cook Time: 35 minutes
Prep Time: 10 minutes
Serves: 6

Ingredients:
1 cup artichoke heart quarters
1 teaspoon lemon juice
1 clove garlic, crushed and minced
¼ cup butter
1 ½ tablespoons flour
1 cup milk, heated
4 eggs, separated

¼ cup Gruyere cheese, shredded
½ teaspoon salt
1 teaspoon white pepper
½ teaspoon nutmeg
1 tablespoon fresh chives, chopped

Directions:

1. Preheat the oven to 400°F and lightly oil a large soufflé pan.
2. Place the artichokes, lemon juice, and garlic in a blender or food processor and blend for 15-20 seconds.
3. Heat the butter in a saucepan over medium heat.
4. Sprinkle the flour into the pan, whisking constantly until a paste forms.
5. Add the milk and whisk until a smooth, creamy sauce forms. Reduce the heat to low and keep warm, stirring frequently to prevent burning and sticking.
6. Place the egg whites in a bowl and beat until firm peaks form.
7. Place the egg yolks in another bowl and beat lightly.
8. Remove the saucepan from the heat and add the artichoke mixture and the egg yolks, whisking quickly to prevent the eggs from scrambling.
9. Add the cheese, salt, white pepper, nutmeg, and chives. Stir gently until the cheese is melted.
10. Carefully fold in the egg whites and gently transfer the mixture to the soufflé dish.
11. Place in the oven and bake for 25 minutes.
12. Carefully remove the soufflé from the oven and serve immediately.

Tomatoes Confites (Baked Tomatoes)

Cook Time: 50 minutes
Prep Time: 10 minutes
Serves: 4

Ingredients:
10 large, ripe tomatoes, cut in half
¼ cup olive oil
1 tablespoon red wine vinegar
3 cloves garlic, crushed and minced
1 teaspoon salt
1 teaspoon coarse ground black pepper
1 sprig fresh rosemary

1 tablespoon fresh thyme
¼ cup fresh parsley

Directions:
1. Preheat the oven to 400°F and generously oil an 8x8 baking dish with 1 tablespoon of olive oil.
2. Place the tomatoes, cut side down, in the baking dish.
3. Drizzle the tomatoes with the remaining olive oil and red wine vinegar.
4. Season with garlic, salt, black pepper, rosemary, thyme, and parsley.
5. Place the baking dish in the oven and bake for 20 minutes. Turn the tomatoes over with thongs or spatula.
6. Reduce the heat to 325°F and bake for an additional 30 minutes.
7. Remove from the oven and serve warm.

Glazed Turnips

Cook Time: 30 minutes
Prep Time: 10 minutes
Serves: 2-4

Ingredients:
3 cups baby turnips, or larger turnips, cubed
2 tablespoons butter
1 teaspoon sugar
½ teaspoon salt
1 teaspoon coarse ground black pepper
1 cup vegetable stock
1 sprig fresh rosemary

Directions:
1. Fill a large saucepan halfway with water and bring to a boil.
2. Place the turnips in the boiling water and blanch for 5-7 minutes. Remove from the water and drain.
3. Heat the butter in a large skillet over medium heat.
4. Add the turnips and season with sugar, salt, and black pepper. Cook, stirring frequently for 3 minutes.
5. Add the vegetable stock and rosemary.
6. Reduce the heat to low, cover, and cook for 15-20 minutes.
7. Remove the cover and continue to cook until the sauce has reduced.
8. Serve the turnips warm, drizzled with the pan sauce.

Sweet French Endings

Mousse au Chocolat(Classic Chocolate Mousse)

Cook Time: 10 minutes
Prep Time: 15 minutes
Serves: 4-6

Ingredients:
1 cup dark chocolate pieces, chopped
8 eggs, separated (only 4 yolks required)
⅔ cup white sugar
¼ cup heavy cream
2 teaspoons brandy
1 vanilla bean, scraped
½ teaspoon finely grated orange zest

Directions:
1. Place the chocolate in a double boiler and melt it over low heat.
2. Place the egg whites in a bowl, together with all but one tablespoon of the sugar, and beat until stiff peaks form. Set aside.
3. In another bowl, combine the 4 egg yolks and the remaining sugar, brandy, vanilla, and orange zest until lightly frothy and creamy.
4. Add the heavy cream to the chocolate, and mix until smooth.
5. Slowly stir the egg yolks into the chocolate, whisking constantly to prevent the eggs from scrambling. Blend until creamy.
6. Remove from the heat, and gently fold in the beaten egg whites.
7. Carefully spoon the mixture into serving dishes, and place it in the refrigerator to chill for at least 2-4 hours.
8. Serve well chilled.

Pear Crepe Cake

Cook Time: 30 minutes
Prep Time: 10 minutes
Serves: 6

Ingredients:
1 ¼ cups almond flour
1 cup all-purpose flour
2 cups milk
4 eggs, lightly beaten
½ cup butter, melted, divided
6 pears, sliced into ¼-inch slices
½ cup sugar
1 tablespoon cognac
¼ cup lavender honey

Directions:

1. In a bowl, combine the almond flour and all-purpose flour.
2. In another bowl, combine the milk, eggs, and half of the melted butter. Mix well.
3. Add the dry ingredients to the wet ingredients and mix just until blended.
4. Heat a crepe pan or small skillet over medium heat and pour a thin layer of the crepe batter into the pan.
5. Cook until small bubbles form and the edges begin to take on a slight golden color. Carefully flip and cook the other side until browned.
6. Remove the crepe from the pan and repeat until all of the batter has been used. Keep the crepes warm.
7. Add the remaining butter to a sauté pan over medium to medium-high heat.
8. Add the pears and sugar and sauté for 1-2 minutes before adding the cognac.
9. Allow the cognac to reduce and continue cooking the pears until they soften and caramelize, approximately 5-7 minutes.
10. Place a crepe on a serving platter and alternate layers of crepes and caramelized pears, making sure to end with a crepe on top.
11. Cut into slices and drizzle with lavender honey before serving.

Classic Tarte Tatin (Reversed Apple Pie)

Cook Time: 70 minutes
Prep Time: 60 minutes plus chilling time for the dough of min. 2 hours
Serves: 8-10

Ingredients:
Dough
1 cup all-purpose flour
2 tablespoons white sugar
½ cup shortening
¼ cup cold water
Vanilla ice cream for serving

<u>Apple filling</u>
6 tablespoons unsalted butter
1 ½ cups white sugar, separated
1 lemon
6 large apple like Golden Delicious

Directions:

1. Using a food processor, add flour, sugar and shortening to the food processor bowl. Pulse a few times. Add the water and continue pulsing until the dough forms. If needed add a tiny bit more cold water at a time. The dough should not be overworked. Remove the dough from the food processor and place on a clean floured working surface. Knead the dough a few times before wrapping with plastic wrap and refrigerate for at least 2 hours and up to 48 hours.

2. In the meantime, Zest and juice the lemon and set aside. Core and peel the apples. Cut the apples into 2 and each half in 4 wedges. Place in a large bowl. Add ½ cup of sugar, le, lemon juice, and lemon zest. Let marinate at room temperature for 30 minutes. Drain the apples.

3. In a large deep ovenproof skillet such as a 9 or 10-inch cast iron skillet, melt the butter over medium-high heat. Add the sugar and stir until completely dissolved. Continue cooking until the mixture turns golden brown. Remove from heat.

4. Layer the apples flat in the skillet following a circular pattern. Place the skillet back on the stove and set heat to medium. Continue cooking covered for 25-30 minutes until the apples are tender. With the back of a spoon, press down on the apples delicately to let the apple juices out. Every 4-5 minutes, baste the apples with cooking juices from the skillet. After 25-30 minutes, the sauce from the apple and sugar mixture should thicken, if not continue cooking covered until it does for a few more minutes. Remove the skillet from the heat.

5. Pre-heat the oven to 400°F and place oven rack in the middle position.

6. On a floured working surface, roll down the dough a bit less than ¼-inch thick and that it covers the whole skillet with 1 extra inch for the sides. Place the dough over the apples, pressing down delicately so that there is limited air pockets. With a sharp knife, cut a few steam holes.

7. Place skillet in the oven and bake for 20-25 minutes or until the crust is golden brown. Unmold on a service plate so that the apples are up and crust is at the bottom. Serve warm with vanilla ice cream if desired.

Mille-Feuilles

Cook Time: 20 minutes
Prep Time: 15 minutes plus chilling time
Serves: 6-8

Ingredients:
1 6-ounce package refrigerated puff pastry dough
4 cups whole milk
2 vanilla beans, scraped
1 ⅓ cups sugar
⅔ cup all-purpose flour
4 eggs, lightly beaten
1 cup confectioner's sugar
½ teaspoon lemon juice
2 teaspoons water
¼ cup dark chocolate, chopped

Directions:

1. Preheat the oven to 400°F and line a baking sheet with parchment paper.
2. Roll the puff pastry dough out into a rectangle measuring approximately 8x16 inches. Cut the pastry into equal thirds.
3. Place the pastry pieces on the baking sheet and lightly poke with a fork over the entire surface. Place the pastry in the oven and bake for 10-15 minutes, or until golden brown. Remove from the oven and let cool.
4. Combine the sugar, flour, and eggs in a saucepan. Whisk until well blended.
5. In a separate small saucepan, heat the milk and vanilla over low heat until steamy. Take ¼ cup of the hot milk and pour it into the sugar and egg mixture, whisking quickly to temper the eggs in the pan.
6. Reduce the heat to low, and slowly add the remaining hot milk, whisking the entire time.
7. Increase the heat to medium and continue to cook, stirring constantly, until the sauce begins to thicken and comes to a very low boil.
8. Remove the custard from the heat and transfer to a bowl. Cover the custard with plastic wrap touching the surface to prevent any air getting to it and forming a skin. Place in the refrigerator and chill for 4 hours.
9. Once the custard has chilled, combine the confectioner's sugar, lemon juice and water in a bowl. Mix until a creamy, but somewhat thin, frosting has formed.

10. Place the chocolate in a small bowl and microwave for 10 seconds to melt, or use a double boiler over low heat.
11. Lay out a third of the pastry dough on a serving dish. Top with half of the custard, followed by a second sheet of pastry.
12. Add the remaining custard on top of the second sheet of pastry and top with the third and final piece of pastry.
13. Spread the frosting over the top of the pastry, letting a little drip down the sides, if desired.
14. Stir the melted chocolate with a knife or thin spatula, and drizzle it in thin parallel lines over the frosting.
15. Using a clean sharp knife or pointed utensil, run a line through the chocolate stripes downward, creating a peaked chocolate pattern over the top of the frosting.
16. Chill if desired, or cut into squares and serve immediately.

Figs in Rosemary Caramel Sauce

Cook Time: 20 minutes
Prep Time: 10 minutes
Serves: 6

Ingredients:
6 fresh figs
1 teaspoon olive oil
1 cup sugar, divided
1 tablespoon lavender honey
2 tablespoons water
1 teaspoon fresh rosemary, finely chopped
1 teaspoon dried lavender flowers, finely ground
1 cup walnuts, coarsely chopped

Directions:

1. Preheat the oven to 400°F.
2. Quarter the figs and brush them very lightly with olive oil. Sprinkle them lightly with one teaspoon of the sugar.
3. Arrange the figs in a baking dish and place in the oven. Roast for 15 minutes. Reduce the oven temperature to 200°F and keep the figs warm while preparing the sauce.
4. Heat the remaining sugar, lavender honey, and water in a saucepan. Heat over medium-low, stirring constantly, until the sugar takes on a light caramel color.
5. Add the rosemary, dried lavender flowers, and walnuts. Mix well.
6. Remove the figs from the oven and arrange on serving plates. Drizzle liberally with the rosemary caramel sauce.
7. Serve warm.

Conclusion

Classical French cooking has a reputation for being incredibly intricate and involved, often suited for the most experienced of chefs. To be fair, in some cases this is true. There are some classic French dishes that require a level of attention that many home cooks simply do not have. However, those few dishes are not a representation of all French cooking, and it is entirely possible to create your favorite bistro dishes in your own home. Some of the dishes included in this book are perfect for a weekend when you have the entire day to devote to creating and perfecting the quintessential French dish, others are simple enough to make for weekday dinner without any advanced preparation. Do you know what these two different styles of dishes have in common? They are both nothing short of delicious and will bring to your table the authentic flavors of your favorite French bistro.

As we fall into the patters of everyday life, it's easy to forget that we are part of a world that is much larger than what we can see outside the front door. This world includes a variety of cuisines, each bringing with it not only the flavors and preparations of the region but also a taste of culture. This book of French Bistro cooking is just one way to bring another corner of the world into your meals, and your life.

More Books from Sarah Spencer

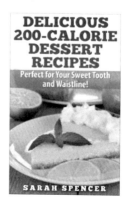

SIMPLE PALEO SALAD
COOKBOOK
50 QUICK & EASY
GLUTEN-FREE SALAD RECIPES
FEEL ENERGIZED, LOSE WEIGHT
AND LOOK HEALTHY
SARAH SPENCER

Gluten Free
TODAY
36 QUICK & EASY LUNCH
AND SNACK RECIPES
SARAH SPENCER

SPICE
IT UP!
THE BEST SPICE MIXING RECIPES FROM
AROUND THE WORLD
SARAH SPENCER

Low Carb
Dump Meals
Healthy One Pot Meal Recipes
Sarah Spencer

Clean
Eating
Made Easy
WHOLESOME CLEAN EATING DIET RECIPES
Feel Healthy · Boost Energy · Lose Weight · Reduce Inflammation
Sarah Spencer

TOTALLY
MEXICAN
CLASSIC AND AUTHENTIC RECIPES FROM MEXICO
SARAH SPENCER

5 Ingredient
Slow Cooker
Recipes
EASY 5 INGREDIENT CROCK POT COOKBOOK
Sarah Spencer

Smoothie
Bowls
50 Healthy Smoothie Bowl Recipes
Sarah Spencer

NO SUGAR ADDED
HEALTHY
FROZEN
DESSERT
Recipes
Ice Pop, Slush, Sorbet, Treat on Stick, Frozen Yogurt,
Frozen drink, Pie, Bar, Parfait and More
LOUISE DAVIDSON

Appendix - Cooking Conversion Charts

1. Volumes

US Fluid Oz.	US	US Dry Oz.	Metric Liquid ml
¼ oz.	2 tsp.	1 oz.	10 ml.
½ oz.	1 tbsp.	2 oz.	15 ml.
1 oz.	2 tbsp.	3 oz.	30 ml.
2 oz.	¼ cup	3½ oz.	60 ml.
4 oz.	½ cup	4 oz.	125 ml.
6 oz.	¾ cup	6 oz.	175 ml.
8 oz.	1 cup	8 oz.	250 ml.

Tsp.= teaspoon - tbsp.= tablespoon – oz.= ounce – ml.= millimeter

2. Oven Temperatures

Celsius (°C)	Fahrenheit (°F)
90	220
110	225
120	250
140	275
150	300
160	325
180	350
190	375
200	400
215	425
230	450
250	475
260	500

49027408R00064

Made in the USA
San Bernardino, CA
11 May 2017